Tracing

Written by Jennifer Dryden
Illustrations by Steve Mack

New York

New York

An Imprint of Sterling Publishing
387 Park Avenue South
New York, NY 10016

ISBN 978-1-4114-5811-6 (paperback)

Distributed in Canada by Sterling Publishing
c/o Canadian Manda Group, 165 Dufferin Street
Toronto, Ontario, Canada M6K 3H6
Distributed in the United Kingdom by GMC Distribution Services
Castle Place, 166 High Street, Lewes, East Sussex, England BN7 1XU
Distributed in Australia by Capricorn Link (Australia) Pty. Ltd.
P.O. Box 704, Windsor, NSW 2756, Australia

For information about custom editions, special sales, and premium and corporate purchases, please contact
Sterling Special Sales at 800-805-5489 or specialsales@sterlingpublishing.com.

Manufactured in Canada
Lot #:
2 4 6 8 10 9 7 5 3
02/12

Dear Parent,

Tracing offers simple and complex tracing activities that progress from straight lines and easy curves to zigzags and loops. These fun exercises build essential fine motor skills and teach your child to follow simple directions. As you work through this book with your child, offer guidance on difficult activities, but allow your preschooler to attempt challenges independently. When the workbook is complete, reward your child with the certificate on page 79. For free downloads and fun activity ideas, visit www.flashkids.com.

Encourage your child to hold the crayon toward the tip to prevent the crayon from breaking. Your child may hold the crayon in his or her fist at first. After a few of the activities, help him or her learn the proper way to hold a crayon.

Sledding is fun!
Trace the path from dot (●) to dot (●).

Scooter feels fancy when he boards a yacht. Trace the path from dot (●) to dot (●).

Help the ambulance drive to the hospital.
Trace the path from dot (●) to dot (●).

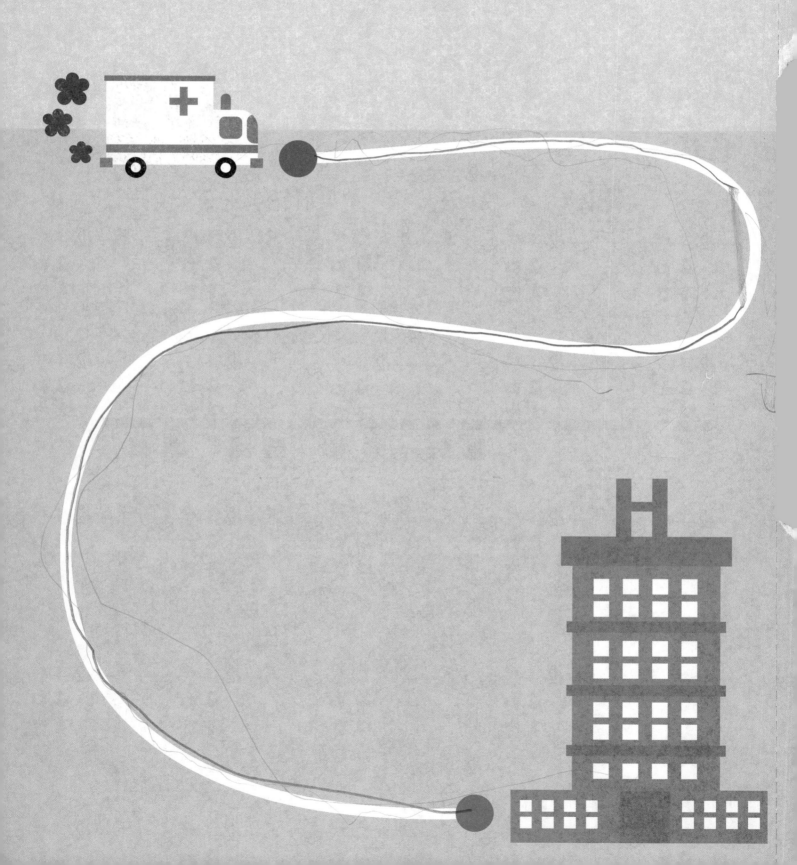

Blimps look like giant balloons.
Trace the path from dot (●) to dot (●).

The man mows the grass.
Trace the paths from dot (●) to dot (●).

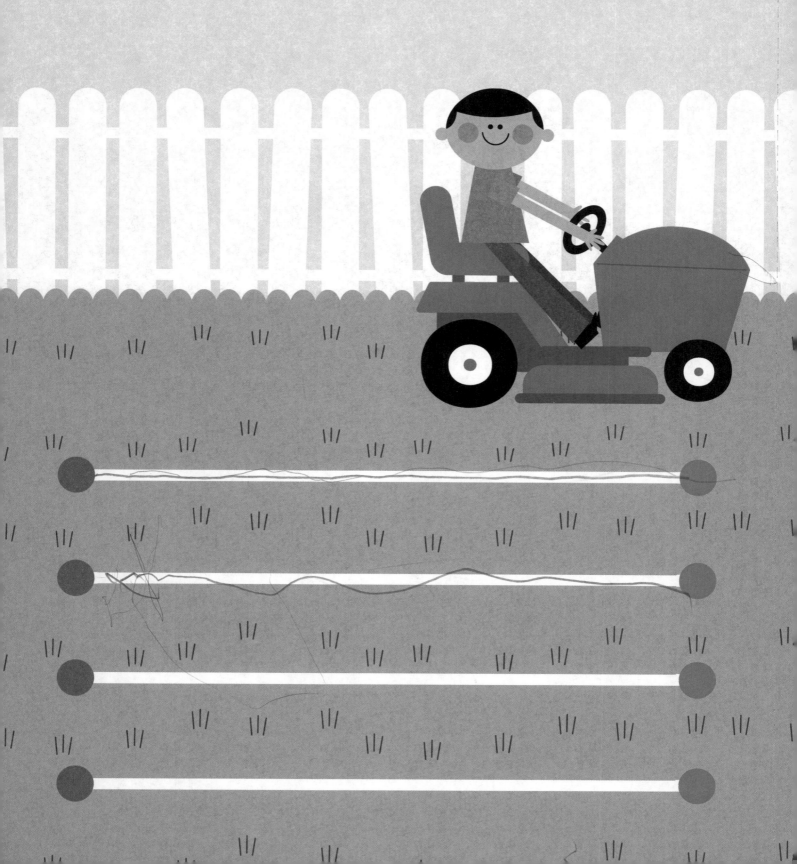

This car looks like a beetle bug.
Trace the path from dot (●) to dot (●).

A hot air balloon floats up, up, and away! Trace the path from dot (●) to dot (●).

These kids strap on their skis and hit the slopes. Trace the path from dot (●) to dot (●).

A pickup truck drives along the dirt road.
Trace the path from dot (●) to dot (●).

The runners jump hurdles.
Trace the path from dot (●) to dot (●).

Scooter flies alongside a helicopter. Trace the path from dot (●) to dot (●).

A crane lifts heavy things.
Trace the path from dot (●) to dot (●).

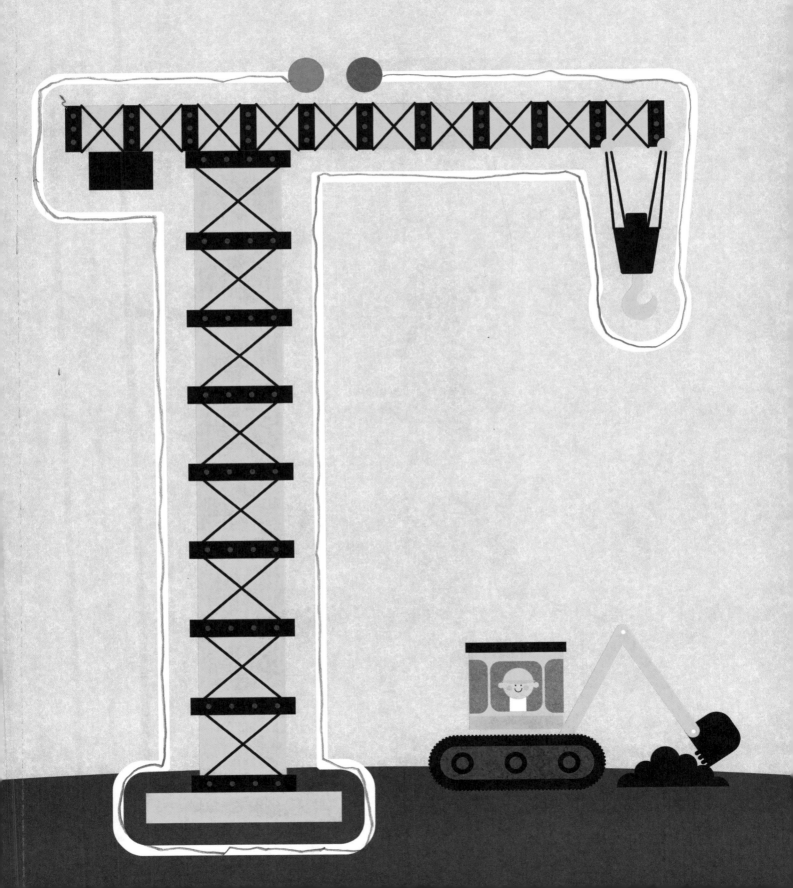

Scooter enjoys a horse-and-buggy ride.
Trace the path from dot (●) to dot (●).

Help the yellow car find a parking space.
Trace the path from dot (●) to dot (●).

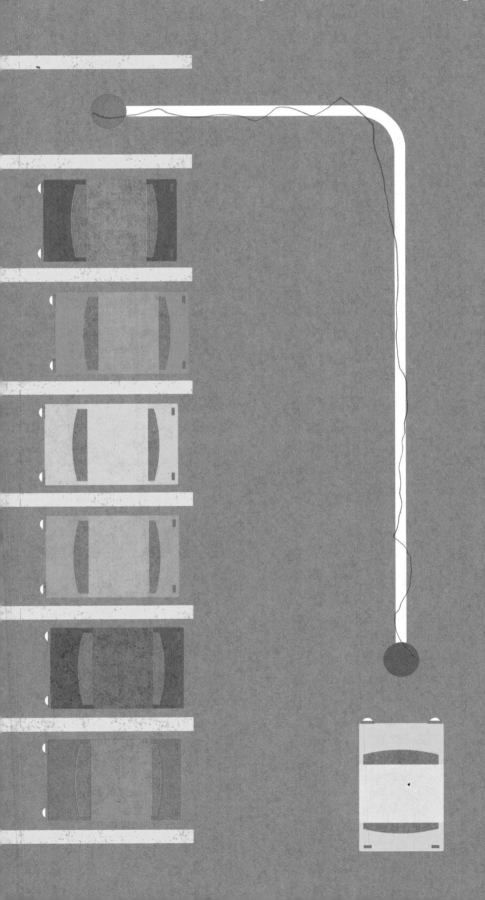
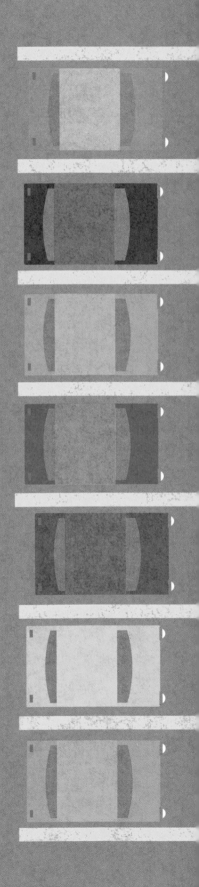

The farmer rides a tractor to tend to his field.
Trace the path from dot (●) to dot (●).

Watch the digger make a giant hole.
Trace the path from dot (●) to dot (●).

Katie moves quickly in her wheelchair. Trace the path from dot (●) to dot (●).

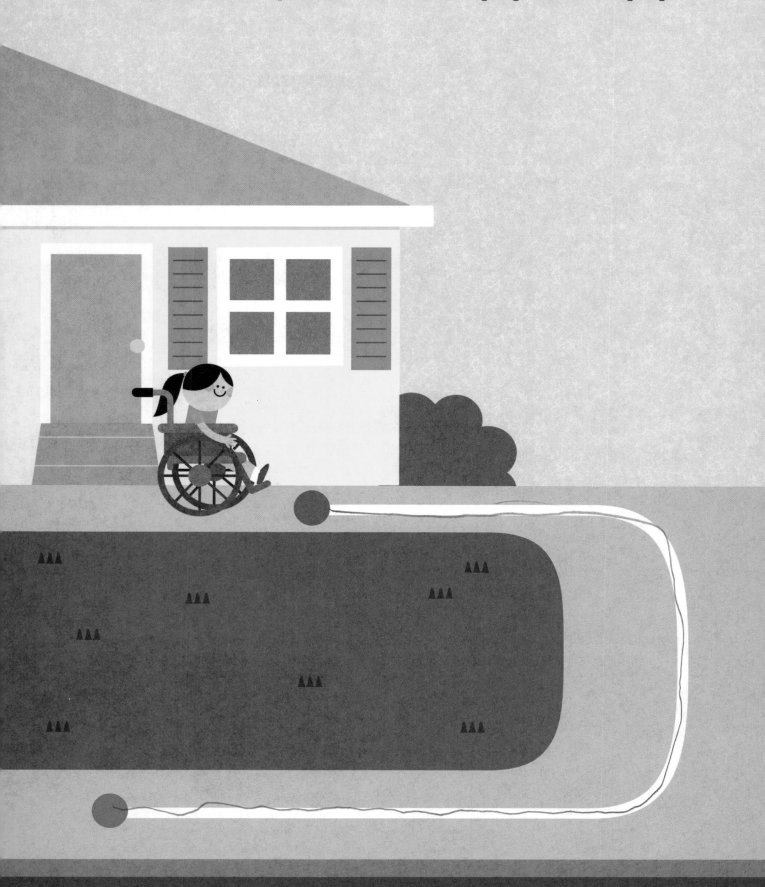

Help the steam engine get to the station.
Trace the path from dot (●) to dot (●).

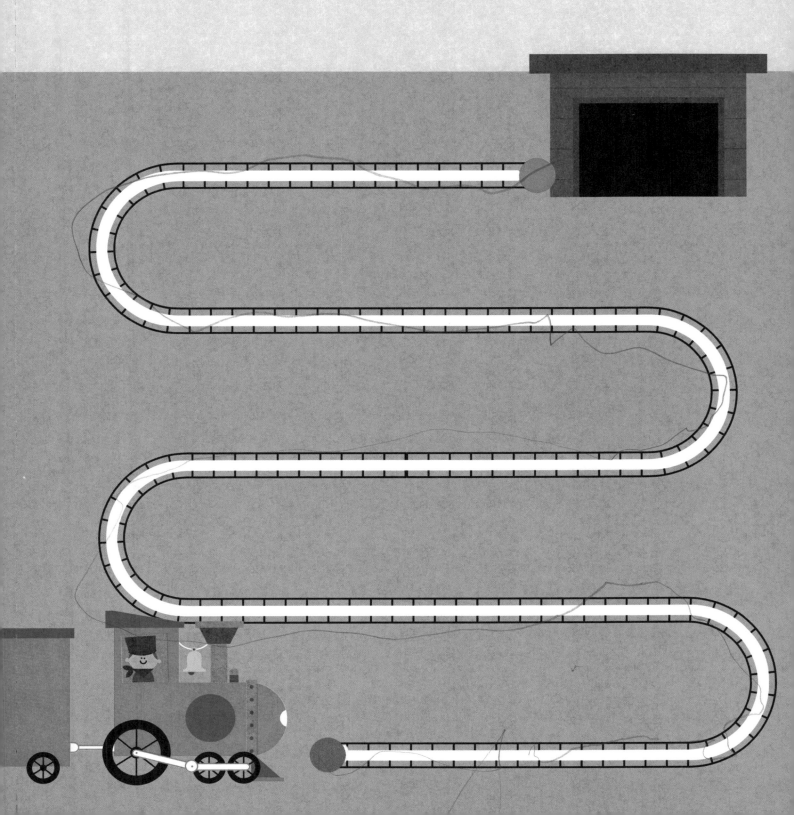

There are a lot of trucks on the highway. Trace the path from dot (●) to dot (●).

Scooter is moving to a new nest!
Trace the path from dot (●) to dot (●).

A snow plow clears a path in the snowy streets. Trace the path from dot (●) to dot (●).

The ferryboat carries people across the river. Trace the path from dot (●) to dot (●).

Convertible cars are fun to drive on sunny days.
Trace the path from dot (●) to dot (●).

Electric cars are good for our planet.
They do not need gas to run.
Trace the path from dot (●) to dot (●).

Safety first! Lifeboats are aboard every ship.
Trace the path from dot (●) to dot (●).

The boy snowboards down a slippery mountain.
Trace the path from dot (●) to dot (●).

Scooter perches on a dock to watch the speedboat. Trace the path from dot (●) to dot (●).

The boy rides his bicycle on the sidewalk.
Trace the path from dot (●) to dot (●).

Scooter loves ice cream!
Trace the path from dot (●) to dot (●).

The police car whizzes by on a high speed chase!
Trace the path from dot (●) to dot (●).

The airplane can fly higher than Scooter.
Trace the path from dot (●) to dot (●).

Walking is a great way to travel!
Trace the path from dot (●) to dot (●).

Scooter is ready for school!
Trace the path from dot (●) to dot (●).

In some cities, people travel by bicycle taxis. Trace the path from dot (●) to dot (●).

Surfing the waves on a surfboard is fun!
Trace the path from dot (●) to dot (●).

Before cars, some people rode horses to town.
Trace the path from dot (●) to dot (●).

Race cars zoom around the track!
Trace the path from dot (●) to dot (●).

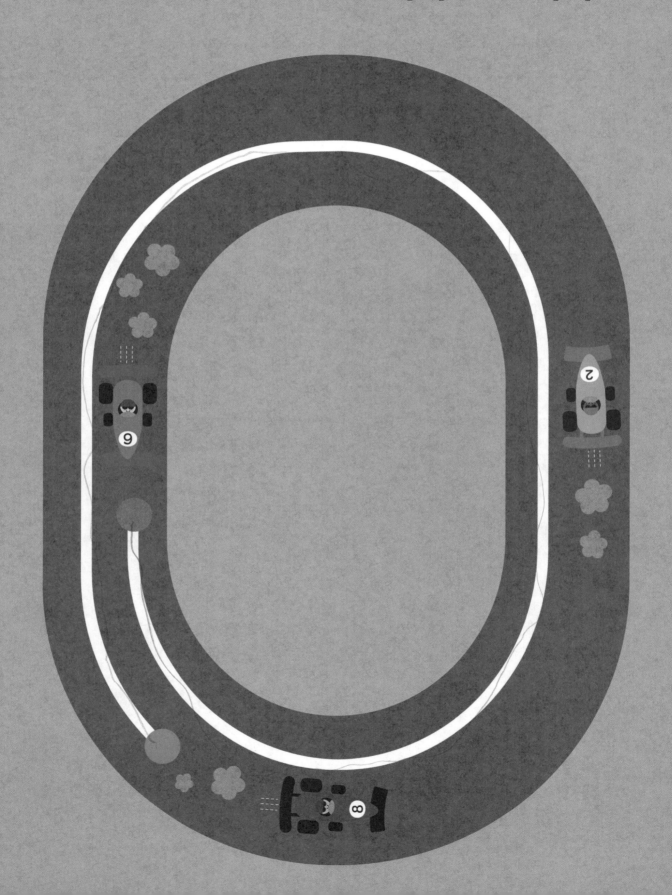

Scooter salutes the army truck.
Trace the path from dot (●) to dot (●).

Combines harvest crops for the farmers.
Trace the path from dot (●) to dot (●).

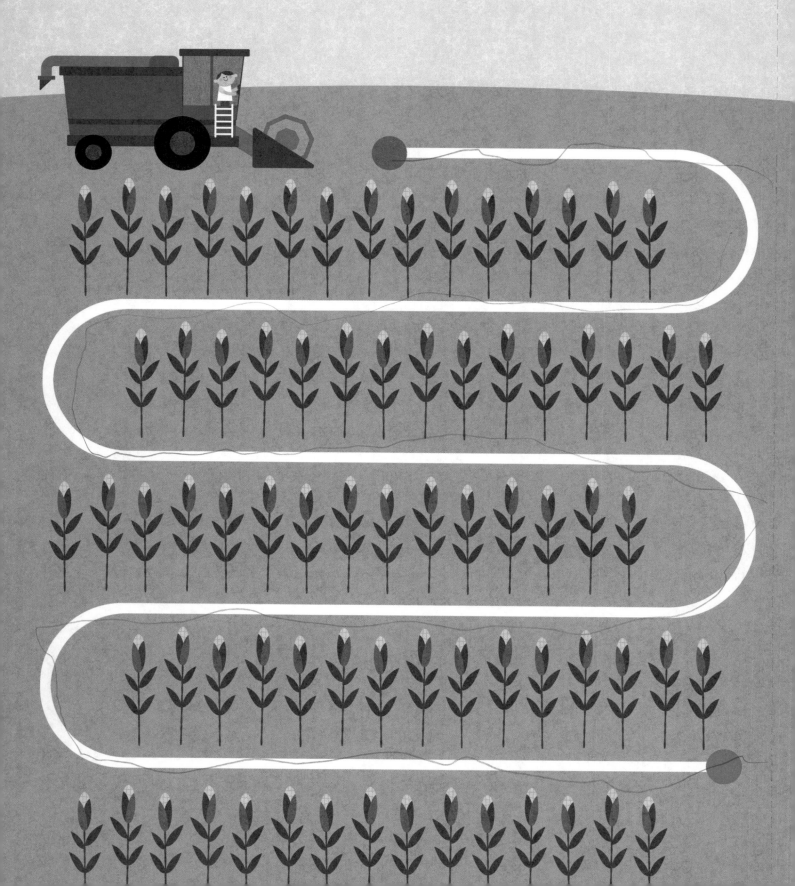

The street sweeper keeps Scooter's town clean. Trace the path from dot (●) to dot (●).

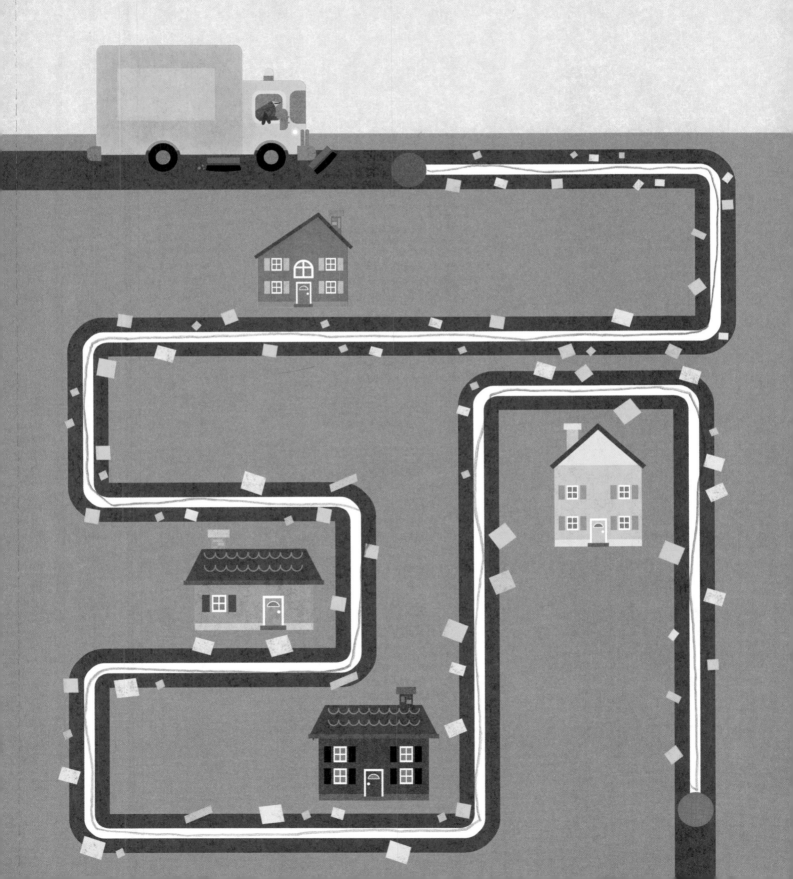

Parasailing is a fun beach activity.
Trace the path from dot (●) to dot (●).

It's tough to balance on a unicycle!
Trace the path from dot (●) to dot (●).

Bulldozers move dirt at construction sites. Trace the path from dot (●) to dot (●).

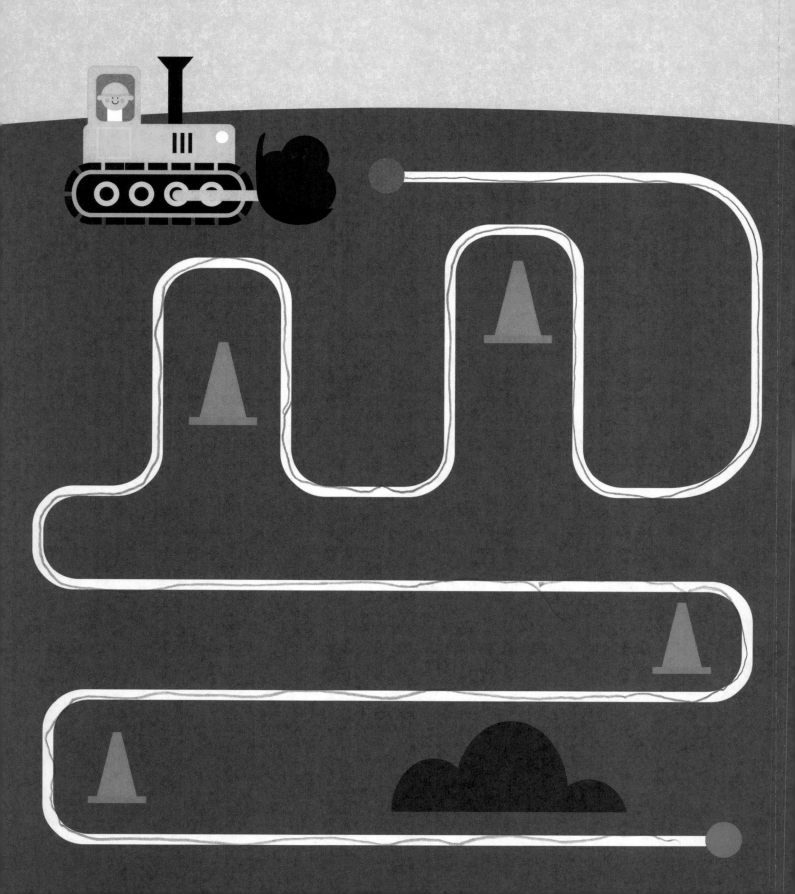

The girl soars through the sky on a hang glider! Trace the path from dot (●) to dot (●).

Scooter wears a helmet on his motorcycle.
Trace the path from dot (●) to dot (●).

In cities, many people ride the subway.
Trace the path from dot (●) to dot (●).

A movie star rides in a limousine.
Trace the path from dot (●) to dot (●).

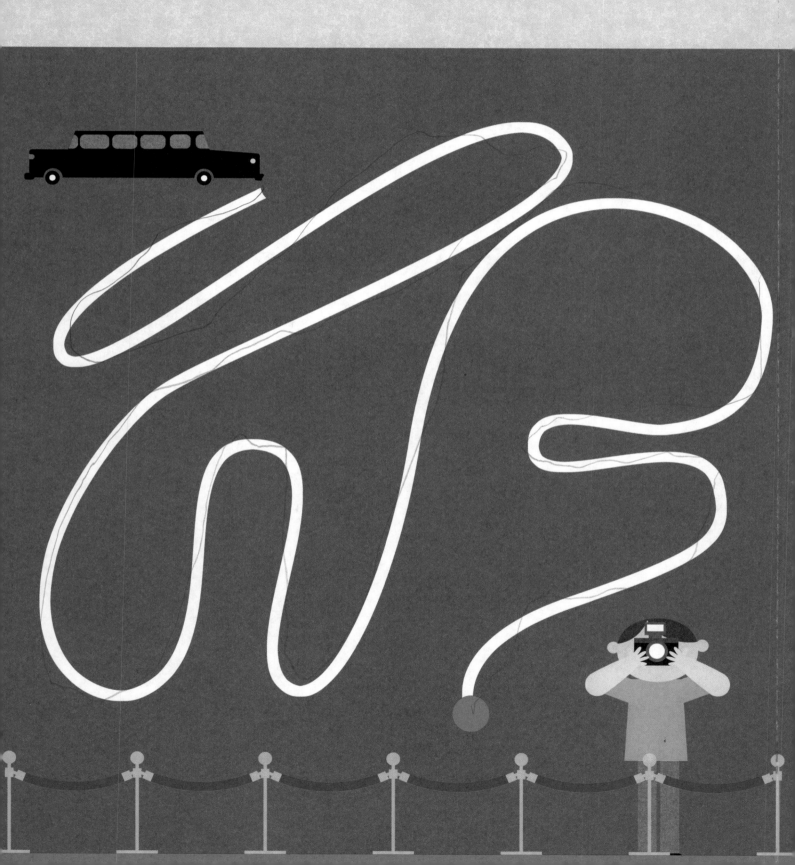

Scooter likes to ride his scooter.
Trace the path from dot (●) to dot (●).

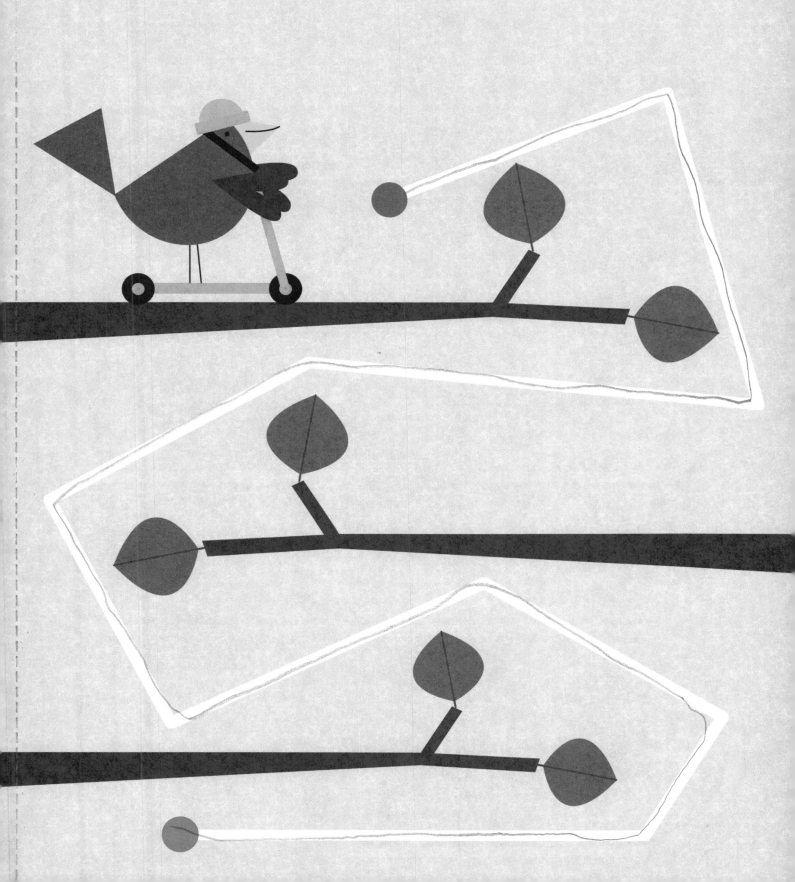

This family drives in a van to the party.
Trace the path from dot (●) to dot (●).

Wearing special snowshoes makes it easy to walk on the snow. Trace the path from dot (●) to dot (●).

There are lots of taxi cabs in big cities. Trace the path from dot (●) to dot (●).

Roller skating in the park is fun!
Trace the path from dot (●) to dot (●).

A fire truck's hose puts out fires!
Trace the path from dot (●) to dot (●).

Take a ride on the beach in a dune buggy!
Trace the path from dot (●) to dot (●).

Trains crisscross over the country.
Trace the path from dot (●) to dot (●).

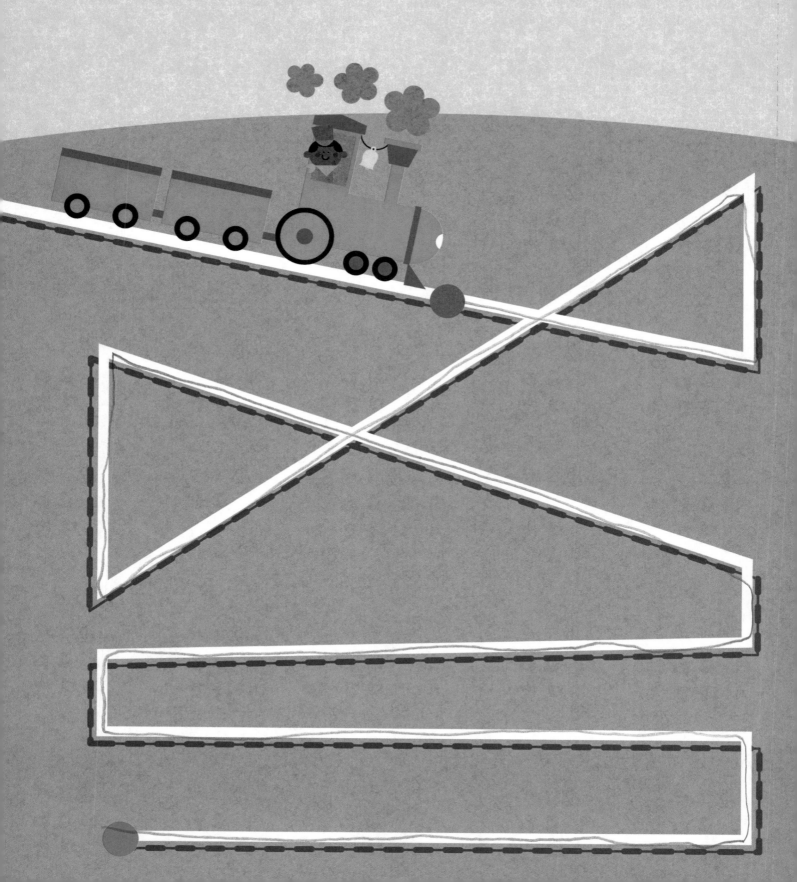

The golf ball flies through the air.
The golf cart follows after it.
Trace the paths from dot (●) to dot (●).

Wind moves a sailboat across the lake.
Trace the path from dot (●) to dot (●).

A dirt bike is used for sport.
Trace the path from dot (⬤) to dot (⬤).

A moon explorer drives on the moon.
Trace the path from dot (●) to dot (●).

How many clowns can fit in a circus car?
Trace the path from dot (●) to dot (●).

Scooter goes deep underwater in a submarine. Trace the path from dot (●) to dot (●).

A dump truck tips its bed to empty the load.
Trace the path from dot (●) to dot (●).

Skateboarders jump, flip, and do neat tricks! Trace the path from dot (●) to dot (●).

An SUV can drive on rough grounds.
Trace the path from dot (●) to dot (●).

Camping in the great outdoors is fun!
Trace the path from dot (●) to dot (●).

The garbage truck brings trash to the dump.
Trace the path from dot (●) to dot (●).

Snowmobiles zip around in the snow.
Trace the paths from dot (●) to dot (●).

Slide down the waterslide!
Trace the path from dot (●) to dot (●).

The mail truck delivers mail each day! Trace the path from dot (●) to dot (●).

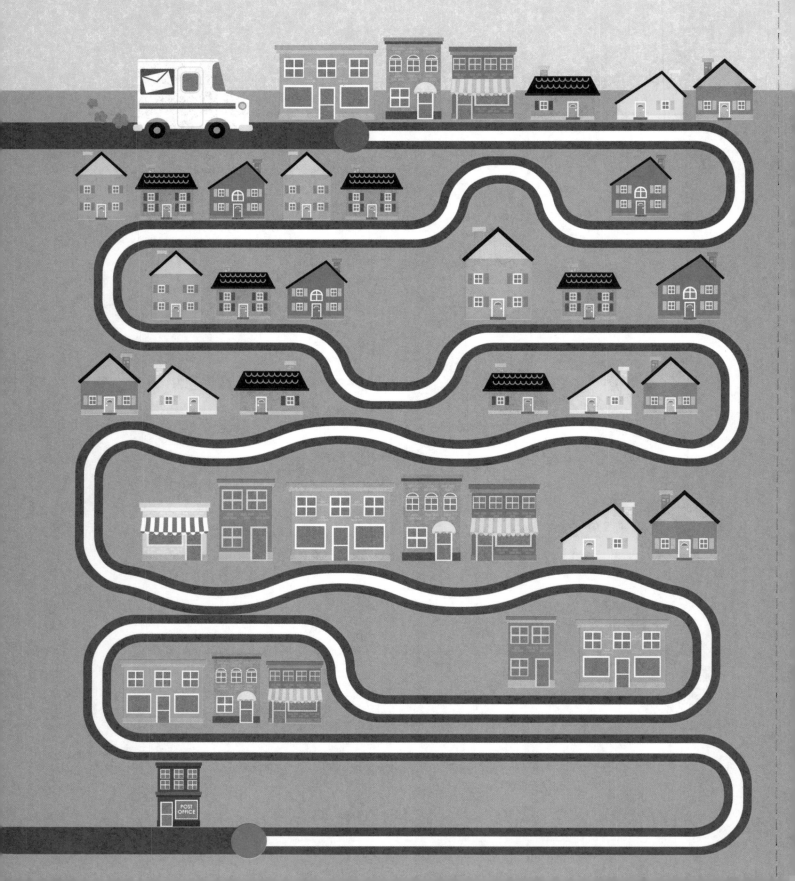

Three, two, one... blast off!
Trace the path from dot (●) to dot (●).

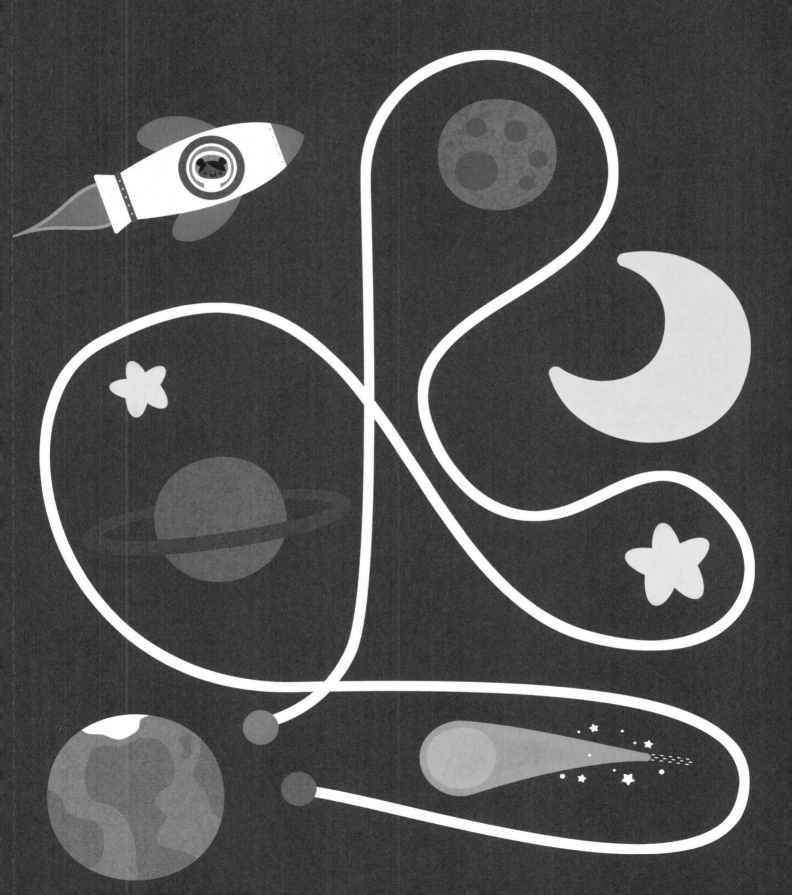

Airplanes do loop-the-loops at the air show. Scooter wishes he could do that, too! Trace the paths from dot (●) to dot (●).

Ride a double-decker bus to see a city's sights.
Trace the path from dot (●) to dot (●).

Scooter rides on top of the remote-controlled car!
Trace the path from dot (●) to dot (●).

These kids whirl and twirl on their ice skates. Trace the paths from dot (●) to dot (●).

Scooter loves roller coasters. They go fast!
Trace the path from dot (●) to dot (●).

Congratulations!

_____

has successfully completed
Tracing.